ALPHABET RHYMES FOR

HALLOWEEN TIMES

By Julie Rae Stitt

DEDICATION

This book is dedicated with love to my grandchildren and those yet to come, in my family, as well as to the children of the world, for the purpose of helping to make learning interesting and fun!

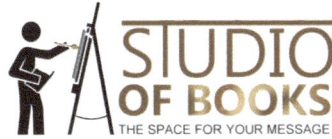

Studio of Books LLC

5900 Balcones Drive Suite 100

Austin, Texas 78731

www.studioofbooks.org

Hotline: (254) 800-1183

Ordering Information:

Special discounts are available on quantity purchases by corporations, associations, and others. For details, contact the publisher at the address above.

Printed in the United States of America.

ISBN-13: Softcover 978-1-968491-55-0
          Hardback 978-1-968491-56-7
          eBook   978-1-968491-57-4

Library of Congress Control Number: 2025917420

A is for apples at Halloween time,

when they're covered with caramel and peanuts – DIVINE!

B is for buckets-

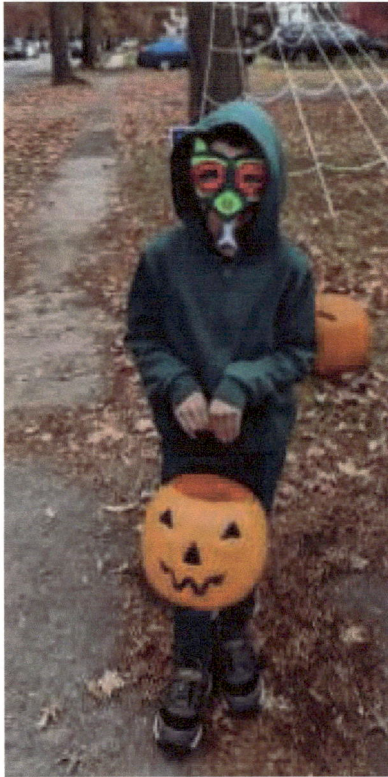

to hold ALL OUR TREATS!

We'll stop at each door, as we go down the streets.

C is for candy that we like to eat.

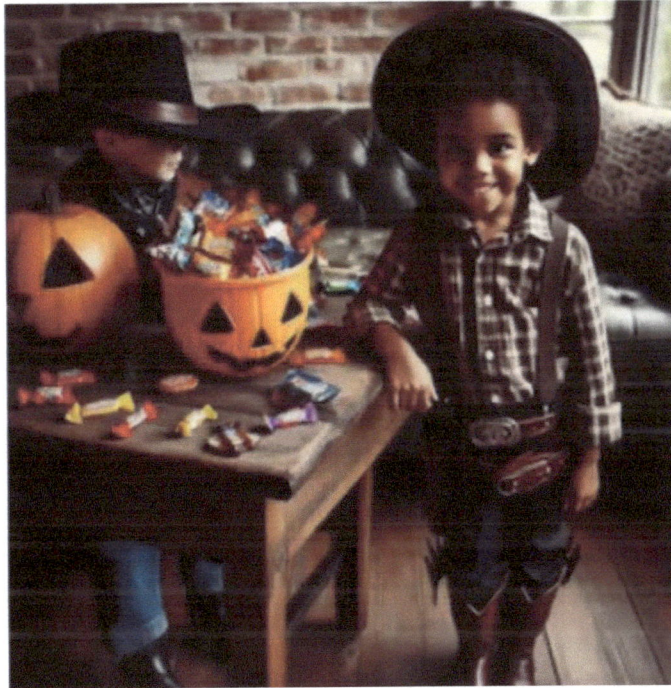

To get so much at once
is really a treat!

D is for dress-up, what we like to do.

BOO!

BOO!

BOO!

**To scare all our friends
we sneak up and say, "BOO".**

E is for excited, the feeling we get.

When it's time to go party,
we are all set!

F is for fun, we'll have some tonight

We'll get candy galore and
give friends a fright!

G is for ghosts that fly through the skies
and goblins so close they look right in your eyes!

7

H is for houses, some *haunted* tonight!

With screeching bats, and witches,

they will give you a fright!

I is for invites your friends like to send.

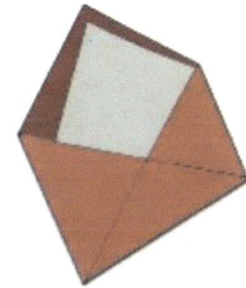

INVITATION
HALLOWEEN PARTY
Date: October 31st Time: 6:00
Dress: Choose your costume!
Address: 27 Spooky Avenue
Scaresville, Haunted Harbor

JOIN US FOR: FUN, FOOD,
CANDY AND GAMES!

Come to play games!
Sure hope you'll attend!!

J is for jack-o-lanterns,
shining so bright.

Carved scary or funny,
they make quite a sight!

K is for kittens, in solid black.

Don't believe they are spooky,
pet their soft, fluffy backs.

L is for lamppost, the place that we meet.

When it's time to go out,
we say, "TRICK OR TREAT!"

M is for monsters in red or in blue.

**But later you'll find out,
they are someone you knew.**

N is for nighttime - what we're waiting for...

to get on
our costumes

and knock
on each door.

O is for ooooooooh and other ghostly sounds

ooooooooooo

oooooooooooo

that come out Halloween Night
and follow you arooound!

P is for pumpkin.

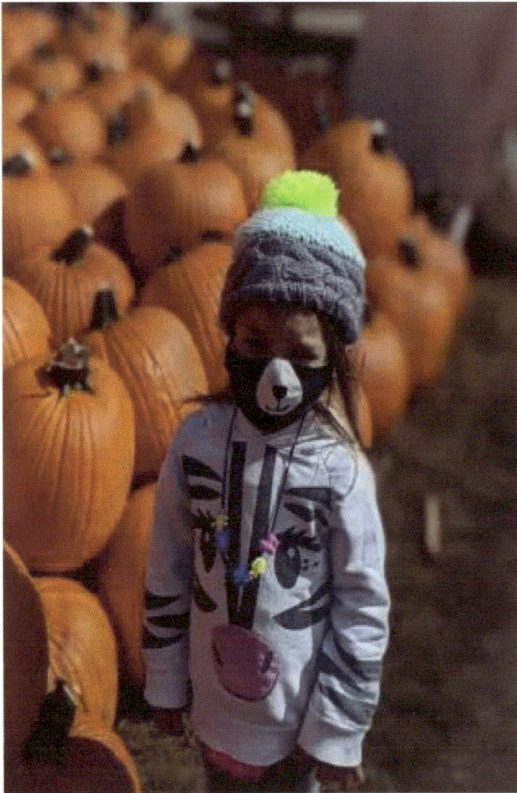

We choose the **BEST ONE**

to take home to carve for Halloween fun!!

Q is for Queen with a crown on her head,

and hearts
on her costume,
all in bright red.

R is for running FAST - door to door!

If we run even faster,
We'll get more and more!

S is for skeletons – look at all of those bones,

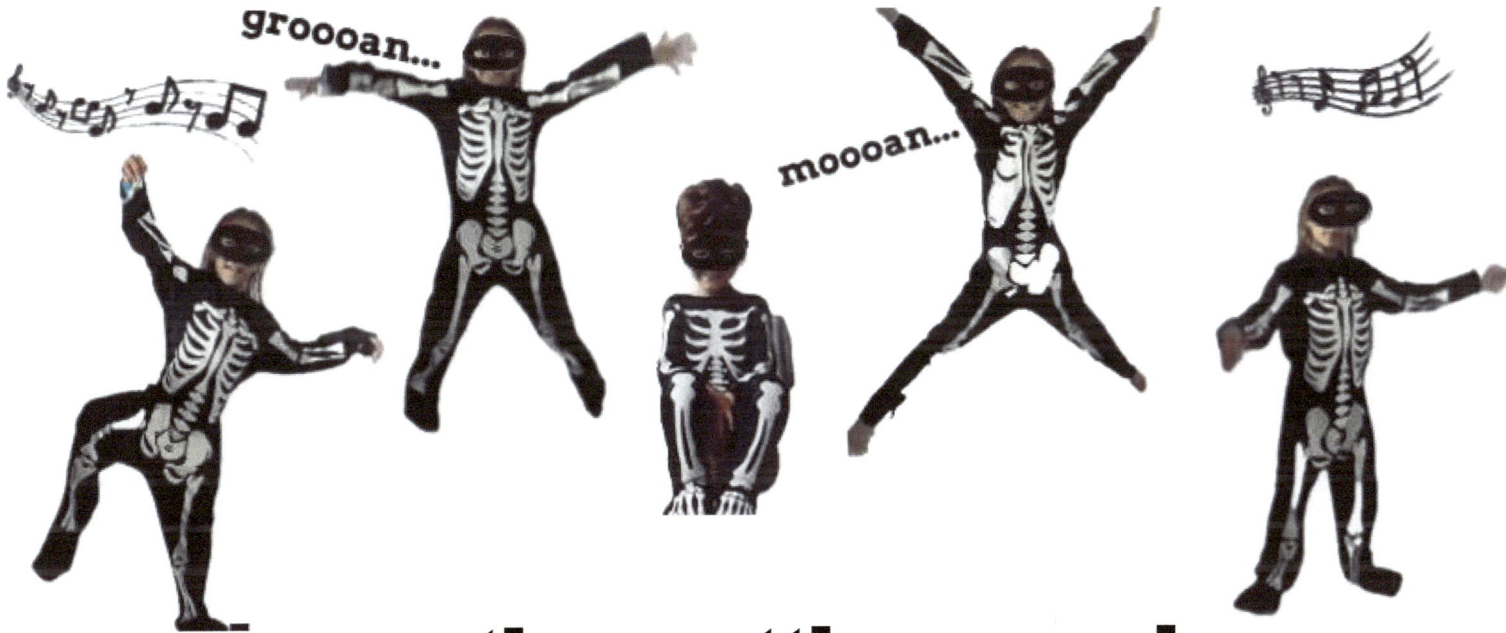

groooan...

moooan...

as they rattle around
and they moan and they groan!

19

T is for "TRICK OR TREAT", words that we yell.

The fact we like candy
is known very well!

U is for ugly, faces that scare.

When they jump up beside you,
stand still, if you dare!

V is for vampire, your neck it might bite.

If it gets very close,
pull your costume up tight!

W is for witches with tall pointed hats,

who ride on their broomsticks,
with solid black cats.

X is for xylophone, whose music we play,

when skeletons
come out and
SCARE people away!

Y is for yell, what we can't help but do,

when we're scared out of our

wits by giant bats, too!

Z is for zombies, who might give you a fright,

but we hope you all have

A HAPPY HALLOWEEN NIGHT!

26

AUTHOR, JULIE RAE STITT

In Julie's career as K-8 teacher, a Certified Prevention Specialist and a Social Worker, she has integrated the use of imagination and the arts as learning tools. Music, creative writing, art and dance have often been incorporated in her teaching life skills to youngsters. Enjoy!

www.ingramcontent.com/pod-product-compliance
Lightning Source LLC
Chambersburg PA
CBHW041551030426

42335CB00004B/185